Actualize!

A STEP BY STEP GUIDE TO CREATING THE LIFE YOU WANT

ACTUALIZE!
Actualize! A step by step guide to creating the life you want

© 2019 Jessica Gifford

Thrive: Growing Wellness, Northampton Massachusetts

Cover and interior design by Isaiah King Design, ikingdesign.com

This title may be purchased in bulk for educational or business purposes. For information, please email jessica@growingwellness.life

Printed in the United States of America

9781095270455

First Printing April 2019

www.growingwellness.life

To actualizers.

Actualizers are people who want to spend our time in more meaningful and fulfilling ways and are ready to explore the possibilities of what that would mean in our lives.

....

Table of Contents

Introduction

Actualize! provides a careful selection of research-based writing exercises to clarify and prioritize what is important to you, and offers step-by-step guidance to help you make positive changes in your life. Each exercise has been chosen based on demonstrated effectiveness in helping people successfully reach their goals. Many also have the happy side effect of improving health, happiness, and productivity. As is true with all impactful practices, the exercises only work if you do them, which is why they have been broken into bite-sized pieces that only take 10-15 minutes each and can be fit into almost any daily routine. I hope you find the process of working through this journal to be enjoyable, meaningful, and rewarding!

Best wishes on your journey,

Jessica Gifford

Is Actualize! for me?

This journal will be particularly helpful to you if one or more of the following is true:

- You want to clarify your life goals, direction, and what is most important to you

- You feel stuck

- You are in transition or are embarking on a new phase of life

- You are working on a challenging goal or project

- You would like to develop a new skill or habit

I'm not sure I'm an actualizer ... what if I don't have any specific goals?

An actualizer is anyone who is in the process of pursuing a more fulfilling life, whether they are engaged in reflection, action, or even confusion! Don't worry if you don't have any well-defined goals or future vision— the process of writing will help you bring your hopes and priorities into clearer focus. Throughout the journal the word "goal" is used to loosely represent your wishes, dreams, the direction you want to go in, what you'd like to accomplish, or the future you'd like to create for yourself. Remember that a goal does not lock you into a specific trajectory. You may change or adjust your goals as your circumstances, priorities or interests change. In this context goals are not limited to achieving specific external markers of success, such as a high income, recognition, or a particular job title. Instead, this journal is designed to help you figure out what you care about most, then put those things front and center in your life.

Actualization truths

In a book about living the life you want, it has to be acknowledged that we do not all have the same opportunities and resources to create positive change in our lives. Some of us have the privilege of having more financial resources and time to pursue the things that matter to us. Some of us have been born into familial and social networks with connections that can help us transform our hopes and dreams into reality. Some of us have been raised to believe that we have the ability to become who we want to become, and to do the things that we want to do. Some of us have received education or other training to develop the necessary skills to achieve these goals.

Unfortunately, many of us do not have these advantages. It is not a level playing field. The odds may be stacked against you based on your race, socioeconomic status, gender, ability, and a number of other factors beyond your control. This is a dispiriting truth. It is also true that we always have some degree of power to create change in our lives and in the world. This journal is intended to provide you with effective tools to help you do just that. In academic settings many of these exercises have been shown to help close the achievement gap between disadvantaged and advantaged students. This offers a glimmer of hope that if we continue to disseminate resources such as this one, and advocate for changes within our institutions, perhaps someday the playing field will level out.

Expected benefits

All of the exercises in this journal are evidence-based, meaning they have been tested and shown to be effective. Some of the benefits you can expect from completing the exercises in this journal include:

- Increased sense of meaning, purpose, and direction

- Greater motivation, follow through, and ability to persevere through challenges

- Higher likelihood of achieving goals

- Improved professional or academic performance

- Decreased symptoms of stress, anxiety, and depression

- Greater happiness and life satisfaction

- Stronger sense of self-confidence and self-efficacy

How to use this journal

This journal is for you. To get the most out of the exercises, find a time and place where you will be able to write without interruption for at least 15 minutes. Please be honest and write freely, without concern for grammar, structure, or spelling. There are no right or wrong answers and no one will be evaluating your responses. It is helpful to give yourself time to reflect on what you've written, so allow at least a day between exercises. If you find you have more to say on a particular topic, you may choose to repeat the same exercise on several consecutive days, filling in additional details or perspectives. You may choose to take more time between exercises, but try to write at least once a week to maintain momentum and progress.

The first five exercises are meant to build upon each other, so it can be helpful to go through them in the order given. However, if there are exercises that you feel drawn to, excited about, or that speak to something that you are going through in the moment, feel free to jump around and do them in whatever sequence is most helpful to you. If you think an exercise may stir up painful or difficult feelings, please use your best judgment about whether or not to do it. Skip it if it is too much right now, knowing you can return to it in the future if you want to.

You are ready to get started. Enjoy!

chapter

1

Preparing

The exercises in this chapter are about reflecting on what really matters to you, prioritizing the things that you care about, and laying a foundation for growth. You will clarify your goals and map out your hopes for the future. Don't worry, you do not need to have any answers to get started, and you can change direction at any time: these exercises are simply meant to reflect your current thinking.

1. Adopt a Mindset for Success

Mission Possible

Attitude isn't everything, but our attitudes fuel our actions, and therefore have a huge impact on whether or not we are successful. If we convince ourselves that we're unlikely to succeed, it becomes easier to give up without even trying. Confidence in your own ability to successfully tackle the challenges you face is referred as self-efficacy. The belief that you have the capacity to learn, grow and change in a particular area is called a growth mindset. This is the opposite of a fixed mindset, or the belief that certain traits, skills, or qualities—such as intelligence, physical abilities, or social skills—are predetermined and unchangeable. Self-efficacy and growth mindset strongly influence your ability to achieve what is important to you, and this exercise helps you develop both.

Benefits

Completing this exercise has been shown to:

- Increase effort and the likelihood of achieving goals

- Protect against stress and build resilience

- Reduce helplessness, anxiety, and depression

Instructions

Please take a moment to think about a specific way that you have grown or changed over time. This could be a challenge or difficulty that gradually became easier, a skill that you developed, or a personality trait or attitude that has changed as you've grown older. Please write freely for about 15 minutes about how you have changed—for the better—in your life. You may choose one specific area to focus on, or write about multiple ways that you have changed. Describe in as much detail as possible what changed and how you made this change happen. What impact has this change or growth had on your life?

_____

_____

_____

What—or whom—helped you to make these changes? Please write about the skills, attitudes, qualities, and support you called upon to make this change.

_____

_____

_____

_____

_____

_____

_____

_____

_____

_____

_____

_____

_____

_____

_____

_____

_____

_____

What would you like to remember from this experience in the future, when you face a challenging situation or important goal? Please write a word or sentence that captures the essence of what you'd like to remember.

_____

_____

_____

How can you remind yourself of this when you need it?

_____

_____

_____

This exercise is based on research by Carol Dweck and David Yeager.

2. Expand Your Perspective
Identify a Larger-Than-Self Goal

This exercise involves reflecting on goals that go beyond personal gain to identify the kind of impact you hope to have on others and on society in general. This may be anything from the effect you have on other people in your daily interactions and relationships, to involvement in a cause, to making a creative contribution. Please be aware of the balance between contributing to others—or a larger purpose—and nurturing yourself. If you are at a point where you feel depleted by giving, you can use this exercise to reflect on how you want to make an impact in a way that also feeds and replenishes you, or you can reflect on the impact that your giving has already had on others. Meaning and purpose can be gleaned from multiple sources, and may change over time. Rather than trying to identify a core life purpose, this exercise provides an opportunity to reflect on what, in this moment, you think might give you a sense of fulfillment in the future.

Benefits

Reflecting on the kind of positive contribution you hope to make to others or society has been shown to:

- Deepen sense of meaning and purpose

- Create greater calmness and well-being

- Reduce depression and anxiety

- Improve academic and work performance

- Strengthen social connections

- Increase persistence through challenges

Instructions

Please write freely for 15-20 minutes in response to these prompts.

Please describe the kind of positive impact you hope to have on others—or on society in general—in the future.

If you prefer, you can write from the perspective of a person or people whom you've had a positive impact on, and describe what they would say about the difference you have made in their lives.

_____

_____

_____

_____

_____

_____

_____

_____

_____

_____

_____

_____

_____

_____

_____

_____

_____

_____

_____

_____

_____

Actualize!

How can your current circumstances (classes, work, family, friends) help you become the kind of person you want to be and have the kind of impact you want to have? How can you make the most of your life right now to create the kind of future you want?

_____

_____

_____

_____

_____

_____

_____

_____

_____

_____

_____

_____

_____

_____

_____

_____

_____

_____

_____

_____

_____

Tip

Did you know that altruistic or compassionate goals, that focus on a greater good, increase positive emotions such as calmness, clarity, connection to others, and overall happiness? If you feel disconnected, discontented, or confused about your direction, it can help to focus on the positive impact you want to have, rather than on how to get ahead.

This exercise is based on research by Jennifer Crocker.

3. Picture Your Future

What do You Want?

In this exercise you will identify all of your hopes and goals in various areas of your life, then prioritize which are currently most important to you. To get the most out of this exercise, it can be helpful to reflect on where your goals come from. The media constantly bombards us with messages about what it means to be successful and these messages often confine us to prescribed gender, class, and cultural roles. You may also have received strong messages from your family and friends about the direction you should take or the kind of life you should live. We are so immersed in family and cultural messages that it can sometimes be hard separate other people's ideas from our own. Trying to live out other people's visions for us may be an easier path, but may ultimately feel empty and unfulfilling. When formulating a goal, it can be helpful to ask yourself,

- Where is this coming from?

- Why is this goal important to me?

- What do I think achieving it will mean to me?

Benefits

This exercise has been shown to:

- Provide a sense of direction and purpose

- Improve organization and time management

- Increase successful achievement of goals

Instructions

Keeping your larger-than-self goal in mind, what do you hope to achieve in each of the following areas? Please imagine your future, and list all of the goals you have in each area.

Educational

_____

_____

_____

_____

_____

Work/career

_____

_____

_____

_____

_____

Personal

_____

_____

_____

_____

_____

Social

_____

_____

_____

_____

Family

_____

_____

_____

_____

Health

_____

_____

_____

Other

_____

_____

_____

_____

Take a moment to look over all of your goals and sort them into the following three categories:

Short-term goals. Of all of the goals you identified, which are the most important to you immediately? Please write down the goals that you'd like to work on in **the next 3 months**.

_____

_____

_____

_____

_____

Mid-range goals. After your short-term goals, what would you like to accomplish within **the next 2 years**?

_____

_____

_____

_____

Long-term goals. Which goals would you like to accomplish in **the next 3-10 years**? These may be lower priority goals that you'd like to defer to a later time, or they may be goals that are highly important to you, but require time to build up to, or are more suited to a later period of your life.

_____

_____

_____

_____

This exercise is based on research by Jordan Peterson. You may find more exercises at selfauthoring.com

4. Visit the Future

Best and Worst Case Scenarios

This exercise involves letting your imagination explore your best possible future, and a future you'd like to avoid.

Benefits

Completing this exercise has been shown to:

- Increase happiness

- Clarify priorities

- Boost motivation and follow-through on goals

Instructions

Please spend a few minutes visualizing your best possible future. Imagine that you have grown into the kind of person you want to be, have built the kind of life that you want, and are able to have the kind of impact on others, or society in general, that you hope for. Create an optimistic—yet realistic—picture of the future. Please spend 10-15 minutes writing continuously, describing your best possible future in detail and incorporating all of the goals you wrote about in exercise 3 (educational, work, personal, family, social, and health goals).

_____

_____

_____

_____

_____

_____

_____

_____

_____

_____

Now please spend 10 minutes writing continuously about a future that you would like to avoid. Create a pessimistic—but possible—version of the future, where things do not turn out the way you hope. Please describe this future life in detail, including the areas of education, work, health, and your personal, family, and social life.

_____

_____

_____

_____

_____

_____

_____

_____

_____

_____

_____

_____

_____

_____

_____

_____

_____

_____

_____

_____

_____

Actualize!

How can you increase the likelihood of creating your best possible future, and decrease the likelihood of the future you'd like to avoid?

_____

_____

_____

_____

_____

_____

_____

_____

_____

_____

_____

_____

_____

_____

_____

_____

_____

_____

_____

_____

_____

_____

_____

Tip

Did you know that mental contrasting, or the act of imagining a hope, goal, or positive outcome, then visualizing potential negative outcomes or obstacles, greatly increases your chances of successfully achieving that goal?

This exercise is based on research by Laura King and Jordan Peterson.

5. Hone In
Clarify Your Focus

Most of the exercises so far have been focused on helping you clarify your goals, or where you want to go in your life. With these goals as your destination, it's time to think about what you need to get there. This exercise involves reflecting on the specific skills and areas of knowledge you need to develop in order to successfully reach your goals.

Benefits

This exercise has been shown to:

- Provide a sense of direction

- Help prioritize and structure time

- Improve academic and work performance

- Increase personal effectiveness

Instructions

Please take a moment to recall your best possible future and your larger-than-self goal. With these in mind, write for about 5 minutes in response to each of the following questions (20 minutes total).

What would you like to learn more about? What skills would you like to improve, or what would you like to become better at?

_____

_____

_____

_____

_____

_____

_____

_____

_____

_____

_____

_____

_____

_____

_____

_____

_____

_____

_____

_____

_____

_____

_____

What habits would you like to improve (academically, at work, with friends or family, related to your health, etc.)?

_____

_____

_____

_____

_____

_____

_____

_____

_____

_____

_____

_____

_____

_____

_____

_____

_____

_____

_____

_____

_____

_____

_____

How would you like to make the most of your time so that you are spending it in a meaningful way, and not wasting it?

_____

_____

_____

_____

_____

_____

_____

_____

_____

_____

_____

_____

_____

_____

_____

_____

_____

_____

_____

_____

_____

How would you like to be described, as a person, by your family, friends, or co-workers?

_____

_____

_____

_____

_____

_____

_____

_____

_____

_____

_____

_____

_____

_____

_____

_____

_____

_____

_____

_____

_____

This exercise is based on research by Jordan Peterson. You may find more exercises at selfauthoring.com

6. Engage Your Strengths

This exercise involves identifying and capitalizing on your core strengths in pursuit of what is important to you.

Benefits

This practice has been shown to:

- Decrease depression

- Increase happiness

- Boost engagement

- Improve academic and professional outcomes

Instructions

Step 1

Identify your strengths. You may list what you see as your top five strengths, or complete a free assessment at authentichappiness.sas. upenn.edu/testcenter to take the VIA survey of character strengths. If you have already completed StrengthsFinder—or a similar assessment tool that identifies your strengths—you may use the results from that. Please list your top five strengths:

1. _____

2. _____

3. _____

4. _____

5. _____

Step 2

Please choose one of your top five strengths, and write freely for 10 minutes about how you can use this strength to help you achieve the things that are important to you.

_____

_____

_____

_____

_____

_____

_____

_____

_____

_____

_____

_____

_____

_____

_____

_____

_____

_____

_____

_____

_____

_____

_____

_____

_____

_____

_____

_____

_____

_____

_____

_____

_____

_____

_____

_____

_____

_____

_____

_____

_____

_____

This exercise is based on research by Martin Seligman. More resources and self-assessments may be found at authentichappiness.com.

7. Check-In

Congratulations! At this point you've spent some time clarifying and prioritizing your goals, the kind of future you want, and the kind of person you'd like to be. Please take a moment to reflect on what you've done, what it has been like, and the impact the exercises have had on you. If you like, you can flip back through the journal to refresh your memory.

What has the process of completing these exercises been like for you?

_____

_____

_____

_____

_____

What progress, if any, have you made toward your goals? What have you learned, or how have you changed as a result of completing these exercises?

_____

_____

_____

_____

_____

_____

_____

_____

_____

_____

_____

How are you feeling about your goals and the progress you are making?

_____

_____

_____

_____

_____

_____

What would you like to say or do to acknowledge, affirm, and celebrate your efforts?

_____

_____

_____

_____

_____

_____

chapter

2

Starting

We often tackle goals with a "just do it" attitude, and try to power our way through—an approach that is rarely successful. This chapter offers well-researched methods for how to make effective progress and successfully achieve your goals.

8. Set a Mini Goal

This exercise involves setting a small goal that you can accomplish in 15-30 minutes, that you will do within the week. Because mini-goals are small, they are easy to achieve, and build a sense of competence and control. Accomplishing a goal triggers a burst dopamine, which generates positive emotion and reinforces forward momentum.

Benefits

Goal-setting has been shown to:

- Help generate movement and momentum

- Reduce inertia, anxiety and depression

- Provide a sense of control and accomplishment

- Prioritize what is important to you

Instructions

Please identify one thing that you would like to do today, or within the week, that can be completed in 15-30 minutes. If you have a larger goal in mind, break it down into small steps and choose one to work on. Please describe your mini-goal:

_____

_____

_____

What made you choose this particular goal? What impact do you think completing will have on you and/or others?

_____

_____

_____

_____

_____

When will you do it?

_____

Where will you do it?

_____

How will you do it? Please describe the steps you will take to complete this goal.

_____

_____

_____

Tip

Did you know that when you choose a goal, thinking ahead to how you will achieve it, and planning the specific details, dramatically increases your probability of success? To turbo-charge your follow-through, specify exactly what you plan to do, and when, where and how you'll do it, then add it to your calendar or set a reminder on your phone. For example, rather than thinking, "I'd like to exercise more this week," write down your plan, "I will go to the gym for a 30-minute workout on Monday, Wednesday, and Friday morning at 8:00 a.m. this week."

9 . WOOP It!

The Magic Formula

This exercise provides a specific structure to increase follow-through and improve the likelihood of successfully achieving your goals. It uses the simple acronym WOOP, which stands for:

Wish: what is your goal? What do you hope to achieve?

Outcome: what will it be like to accomplish the goal? What impact will it have on your life?

Obstacle: what could get in your way?

Plan: what will you do to overcome these obstacles?

Benefits

This exercise has been shown to:

- Increase follow-through on goals

- Build effectiveness in overcoming challenges

- Increase the likelihood of successfully achieving goals

Instructions

Wish: What is your goal? Please choose something that you would like to focus on within the next 3 months. What do you hope to achieve?

_____

Outcome: What would it mean to accomplish this goal? Please write in detail for 5 minutes about how accomplishing this goal would affect all areas of your life. What would it look like? How would it feel? How would it affect your family and friends?

_____

_____

_____

_____

Obstacle: What could prevent you from achieving this goal? Please write for 5 minutes about the main internal obstacle that holds you back. This could be an emotion, a negative belief, or a bad habit. Describe the obstacle as specifically and in as much detail as possible.

_____

_____

_____

_____

_____

_____

_____

_____

_____

_____

_____

_____

_____

_____

_____

_____

_____

_____

_____

Plan: What will you do to overcome this obstacle? Please create an if-then plan such as, "If I feel tired, then I will remind myself why this is important to me and do it anyway."

_____

_____

_____

_____

_____

_____

_____

_____

_____

_____

_____

_____

_____

_____

_____

_____

_____

This exercise is based on research by Gabriele Oettingen. More information and resources can be found at woopmylife.org.

10. Make it Manageable!

This exercise helps you turn large, vague goals into clearly defined, achievable steps.

Benefits

Making goals manageable and actionable has been shown to:

- Reinforce momentum and accelerate progress

- Increase the likelihood of achieving goals

- Increase productivity and effectiveness

Instructions

Step #1: Break it down

People are far more likely to achieve big goals when they are broken down into smaller, well-defined action steps. Please choose a medium or large-sized goal you are working towards—and list all of the small action steps necessary to complete it.

1. _____

2. _____

3. _____

4. _____

5. _____

6. _____

7. _____

8. _____

9. _____

10. _____

Do these action steps need to be completed in a particular order? If so, please list them in sequence.

1. _____

2. _____

3. _____

4. _____

5. _____

6. _____

7. _____

8. _____

9. _____

10. _____

Step #2: Do Less

We are often overly enthusiastic in setting goals, only to feel daunted by the effort required to follow through on them. When you have multiple goals, or big goals, it's helpful to focus on one or two things at a time, and start with small easy steps that you can gradually build on. If you fail to follow through on a step you've set for yourself, break it down into something more manageable. Unfortunately, we often do the exact opposite, raising the stakes and making the task even more difficult to tackle, for example, "Since I didn't go to the gym today, I'll do double my workout tomorrow." Remember that early success reinforces momentum, so start small! In fact, plan to do less than you want to. Please choose one of the action steps that you identified above that you would like to work on. Describe what you think you can realistically get done on this step this week.

_____

_____

_____

Now describe what this would look if you cut it in half, or pared it down to a 10-minute task.

_____

_____

_____

On a scale of 1-10 how confident are you that you will accomplish this goal? 1 = completely lacking in confidence and 10 = total confidence

1   2   3   4   5   6   7   8   9   10

If you are less than an 8, consider doing less, or choosing a different step.

Step #3: Visualize!

Visualization can be a powerful tool when used correctly. However, visualizing or daydreaming about reaching your goal can actually make you less likely to take action because visualization tricks your mind into thinking you've already accomplished the desired outcome. You can overcome this by visualizing your ideal outcome and then mentally contrasting it with the potential obstacles to achieving it, as you did in Exercises 4 and 6. Another strategy is to visualize the process of achieving the goal, rather than the outcome. By mentally walking through each of the steps you will take, you prepare yourself for action. This increases follow-through and performance, and is especially effective when you are doing something that is unfamiliar or anxiety-provoking, such as a presentation or job interview.

Please take a moment to visualize when, where, and how you will accomplish the action step you've identified.

When will you do it?

_____

_____

Where will you do it

_____

_____

How will you do it?

_____

_____

_____

Tip

Did you know that fewer than one in ten people successfully keep their New Year's resolutions? One of the main reasons people fail is that they are too ambitious. There is nothing wrong with having an aspirational goal, called a "stretch goal"—in fact, a stretch goal can inspire you and provide a sense of direction. However, breaking a stretch goal down into small, achievable steps will dramatically improve your chances of success.

11. Harness the Power of Habit

This exercise involves identifying a positive action or behavior and working to establish it as a habit. When we create a habit we put a specific behavior on autopilot, dramatically reducing the amount of effort needed to carry it out. Habits are formed through repetition and through linking the behavior to specific cues. For example after I wake up (cue) I will make coffee (cue), then I will write for twenty minutes (cue), then I will brush my teeth. Once the behavior becomes ingrained there is little need for thought, decision-making, or planning.

Benefits

Turning a behavior into a habit has been shown to:

- Reduce the amount of effort and willpower necessary to perform a desired behavior

- Increase successful goal achievement

Instructions:

Please take a moment to reflect on your short- and long-term goals. Now choose a specific behavior that you would like to automatize and practice on a regular, or daily basis.

_____

_____

_____

What impact would it have on you to create this new habit? Please write a short motivational statement about why this habit is important to you that you can refer to anytime your motivation flags.

_____

_____

_____

Step 1: Identify a Cue.

A cue can be a specific time of day, for example, every night before I go to sleep I will write three things I am grateful for. A cue may be an already established habit, for example, after I brush my teeth (cue) I will floss. A cue may also be a visual reminder, for example, when I see the vitamins next to the coffee maker each morning, I will take one. It is important for cues to be clear and obvious.

What cue will you use to prompt you to engage in your new habit?

_____

_____

When will you do it? Please choose a specific time of day, and specific days of the week (if not every day) that you will engage in your habit.

_____

_____

Where will you do it?

_____

Step 2: Make it Easy.

We are drawn toward the path of least resistance, so it is important to make new behaviors easy to engage in. Rather than attempting to practice an entire new behavior at once, it can be effective to break your habit into incremental steps, and get the first step well-established before moving on to the next. For example, if you want to learn guitar, you could start with simply getting the guitar out of its case and putting it on your lap at the same time each day, without playing anything. This may seem like an odd practice, but it helps to ingrain the first step of a new habit, which can then serve as the cue for the next step. It is also important to set up your environment to make your habit easy to engage in, for example, by leaving your guitar in the living room rather than tucked away in a closet.

How will you make your new habit easy to engage in?

_____

_____

_____

_____

Step 3: Make it Enjoyable.

We are far more likely to want to engage in activities that are enjoyable to us. If a new behavior isn't inherently enjoyable or rewarding, it is possible to make it more appealing by linking it with something you like doing, for example only allowing yourself to watch a favorite show while working out. It can also be effective to gamify the behavior by setting challenges or rewards for yourself. You may look forward to activities more if you do them with friends or in an environment you enjoy.

How can you make your new habit enjoyable?

_____

_____

_____

_____

Tip

Did you know that willpower is a limited resource that tires like a muscle? If you rely on willpower alone to get through what you need to do to achieve your goals, you are more likely to wear yourself out and give up. By sticking to a regular routine, the action or behavior gradually becomes ingrained, until you eventually perform it on autopilot, bypassing mental debate and struggle. Some habits—particularly those that are enjoyable and accompanied by a burst of dopamine—are easy to establish, such as a morning cup of coffee. Habits that you know are good for you, but aren't particularly fun, take more time to become ingrained, such as flossing every night. The longer you stick with it, the easier it will become. You can reverse the three steps above to help you break bad habits: remove cues, make it hard, and make it unpleasant.

12. Track it!

Tracking a behavior provides valuable information, allowing us to benchmark our starting place and assess progress toward a goal. Noticeable progress fuels motivation and reinforces momentum. Tracking can also provide accurate and immediate feedback, which is crucial to improving skills, as it lets us know what is working and what isn't. Tracking is equally powerful when you are working to increase a behavior, such as counting your daily steps, or when you are working to decrease a behavior, such as counting the number of cigarettes you smoke each day.

Benefits

Tracking a behavior has been shown to:

- Accelerate skill development

- Increase successful behavior change and achievement of goals

Instructions

Please choose an area of your life that you would like to get a feedback on, or a behavior you would like to increase or decrease. What would you like to track?

_____

_____

How will you track it? Tracking can include keeping a journal, marking your calendar, using a tracking app, counting a specific behavior, etc. Please be specific about what you will do and when you will do it.

_____

_____

_____

13: Identify Your Supports

The focus of this exercise is to identify and connect to supports and resources to help you overcome hurdles and accelerate progress. The bigger and more challenging the projects or goals you're working on, the more crucial it is to seek support.

Benefits

Enlisting the help of others has been shown to:

- Speed up learning and progress toward goals

- Increase accountability and follow through

- Make the process of working on goals more enjoyable

Instructions

Please take a moment to reflect on the goals you've identified and your current focus. Would additional encouragement, accountability, or resources help you move forward? Please choose an area that you could use help with and describe it as specifically as possible.

_____

_____

_____

_____

Support can take many forms. It is important to reflect on what would best suit your needs and personality.

Cheerleaders

These are the people who see the best in you, believe in your ability to succeed, and are there to offer you support when you need it. If a cheerleader is not available, you can also call on the internalized voices of loved ones who have passed away, or inspirational figures, for example, "What would my grandmother do or say in this situation?"

Who are the cheerleaders in your life? Who you can turn to when you need encouragement?

_____

_____

_____

_____

How can you call on your cheerleaders to help you move forward on the things that you care about?

_____

_____

_____

Buddies

These are the people who are working on the same goal as you, and reinforce your efforts by providing companionship, support and shared experience. Buddies are effective because we tend to enjoy time with others more than time alone, and it is much harder to back out of a commitment to someone else than it is to break a promise to ourselves. Buddies can be friends, or can be found in classes or groups.

Would a buddy be helpful to you right now? If so, please identify possible buddies, groups or classes that would support your progress:

_____

_____

_____

_____

How and when will you establish a buddy relationship or enroll in a class or group?

_____

_____

_____

Accountability partners: These are people who you regularly check in with about your goals and progress. For example, you may set a goal of writing one page per day and set a weekly check-in time with a friend, coach, or colleague whom you've asked to be your accountability partner. Sharing your goal and knowing you need to report back on it boosts motivation and follow through.

Would an accountability partner be helpful to you right now? If so, who are possible accountability partners that you could regularly check-in with about each other's goals?

_____

_____

_____

_____

How and when will you reach out to potential accountability partners?

_____

_____

_____

Professionals

These are people who have expertise, or an area of specialization that can accelerate your progress. Professionals can offer valuable information, feedback and advice, teach specific skills, and help you make connections. If you can afford it, it can be well worth it to outsource specific tasks to professionals, such as hiring a web designer to create your website instead of spending hours trying to do it yourself, or employing a coach to work on your public speaking skills.

Would a professional be helpful to you right now? If so, what specifically would you like a professional to help you with?

_____

_____

_____

_____

_____

How and when will you reach out to professionals?

_____

_____

_____

14. Check-In

Congratulations, you're halfway through the journal! You have worked to clarify what's important to you and have learned some strategies to help you effectively follow through on your goals. Please take a moment to think back over what you've done, what it's been like, and the impact the exercises have had on you. If you like, you can flip back through the journal to refresh your memory.

What has the process of completing these exercises—and working toward your goals—been like for you?

_____

_____

_____

_____

_____

What progress have you made toward your goals? What have you learned, or how have you changed as a result of the work you are doing?

_____

_____

_____

_____

_____

_____

_____

_____

_____

_____

How are you feeling about your goals and the progress you are making?

_____

_____

_____

_____

_____

What would you like to say or do to acknowledge, affirm, and celebrate your efforts?

_____

_____

_____

chapter

3

Overcoming

Pursuing what is important to you is a rewarding and meaningful path, but it is not always an easy one. Challenges, set-backs, and disappointments are inevitable, and they present pivotal moments that we can respond to by giving up, or by digging deeper. The exercises in this chapter provide evidence-based strategies to work through difficulties and continue to focus on what really matters to you.

15. Set a Mini Goal

This exercise involves setting a small goal that you can accomplish in 15-30 minutes, that you will do within the week. Because mini-goals are small, they are easy to achieve, and build a sense of competence and control. Accomplishing a goal triggers a burst dopamine, which generates positive emotion and reinforces forward momentum.

Benefits

Goal-setting has been shown to:

- Help generate movement and momentum

- Reduce inertia, anxiety and depression

- Provide a sense of control and accomplishment

- Prioritize what is important to you

Instructions

Please identify one thing that you would like to do today, or within the week, that can be completed in 15-30 minutes. If you have a larger goal in mind, break it down into small steps and choose one to work on. Please describe your mini-goal:

_____

_____

_____

What made you choose this particular goal? What impact do you think completing will have on you and/or others?

_____

_____

_____

_____

_____

When will you do it?

_____

Where will you do it?

_____

How will you do it? Please describe the steps you will take to complete this goal.

_____

_____

_____

16. Change Your Self-Talk

Noting Practice

We all engage in ongoing mental commentary about ourselves and what is happening around us, whether we are fully conscious of it or not. Self-talk includes narratives about the kind of people we are, what we like and don't like, and evaluative judgments about our thoughts, feelings, and behavior. Critical, pessimistic, or otherwise negative self-talk undermines confidence and impedes our ability to move forward. It is one of the biggest obstacles to becoming the kind of person you want to be and living the kind of life you want to live. This exercise guides you through mindful noting practice to neutralize negative thoughts.

Benefits

Mindful noting practice has been shown to:

- Reduce anxiety and depression and improve mood

- Improve performance

- Increase persistence and achievement of important goals

- Improve self-concept

Instructions:

Mindful noting practice can be used anytime you experience negative thoughts and emotions. For this particular exercise, please focus on any anxieties, self-judgements, or difficult emotions that come up related to pursuing your goals. This exercise entails following the three simple steps, Notice, Accept, and Narrate (NAN).

1. Notice

Take a deep breath, and bring your attention to what you are thinking and feeling. Please list all of the thoughts and feelings—both positive and negative—that have recently surfaced in response to working on your goals. Try to note your thoughts and feelings without judgment, as if you were a neutral observer.

_____

_____

_____

_____

_____

_____

_____

2. Accept

Take a deep breath. Instead of trying to suppress, change, or argue with your thoughts and feelings, practice accepting them no matter how uncomfortable they may be. Please describe how it feels to practice acceptance.

_____

_____

_____

_____

3. Narrate

Name whatever you are thinking and feeling in a neutral, nonjudgmental tone. It may be helpful to narrate from a second or third-person point of view. For example, "You're feeling tense and angry and you're thinking this isn't fair." This creates more distance from your thoughts and emotions and will help you detach from them.

_____

_____

_____

_____

_____

_____

_____

_____

Tip

Did you know that trying to suppress or deny thoughts and emotions only makes them stronger, and they last longer? Mindfulness is an effective practice because it teaches us to accept whatever thoughts and feelings we are having in the moment.

17. Practice Self-Compassion

When the Going Gets Tough, the Tough Get Compassionate

This exercise offers an effective tool to get through the emotional rough patches that inevitably arise, and that have the potential to derail you from pursuing your goals.

Benefits

Practicing self-compassion has been shown to:

- Improve mood, reduce depression and anxiety

- Increase connection to others

- Build confidence and positive self-image

- Speed recovery from setbacks and difficulties

- Increase persistence and the likelihood of goal achievement

Instructions:

Step 1:
Identify a positive, compassionate voice. This could be:

- A friend, relative, or mentor who consistently sees the best in you

- An inspirational figure whom you respect and admire, whether alive or deceased

- An imaginary or mythical figure, such as a superhero, a spirit guide, or the character of a book or movie

- Your future self

Please describe the owner of the positive voice. Who (or what) are they?

_____

_____

_____

Step 2

Choose a specific situation that is creating stress or suffering for you in relation to pursuing your goals. Please choose a situation that is big enough that it is significantly affecting you, but not so big that you don't feel like you can handle it right now. Imagine that the owner of the positive voice is observing your experiences, thoughts, and feelings. Now please write from their perspective and describe all of your feelings and thoughts in a tone that is validating and nonjudgmental. It is not necessary to describe the situation itself, just identify the thoughts and emotions that it triggers as thoroughly as possible.

_____

_____

_____

Step 3

Next, please take a moment to bring to mind other people—known and unknown to you—who have had similar experiences and emotions to the ones you are going through right now. Remind yourself that what you are going through is part of the human experience. Please write for a few minutes about your empathy, understanding, and compassion for all of the other people in your community, or in the world, who have shared similar experiences and emotions, and how this connects you with them. You may also use phrases like, "This is part of the human experience" or "This is part of being a (parent/activist/artist)."

_____

_____

_____

_____

_____

_____

_____

_____

_____

Step 4

Finally, from the perspective of the positive voice you have identified, please offer yourself words of kindness, guidance, and support. What words of encouragement would bolster your spirit?

_____

_____

_____

_____

_____

_____

_____

_____

_____

_____

_____

_____

_____

_____

Tip

Many people think that self-criticism is motivating, that if they are too easy on themselves, they'll become lazy. In fact, the opposite is true. Self-compassion does contribute to greater tolerance for making mistakes, but this does not lead to complacency or sloppiness. Instead, the reduced fear of failure frees self-compassionate people to take more risks, and increases the likelihood they will persist toward—and accomplish—important goals.

This exercise is based on research by Kristin Neff. More self-compassion practices can be found at selfcompassion.org

18. Be a Scientist

Setbacks and missteps are an inevitable part of working toward something important. How we respond to setbacks is predictive of whether or not we will continue to pursue our goals or give up. This exercise offers strategies on how to move beyond the initial disappointment and frustration after a setback, and explore opportunities for learning and growth.

Benefits

Looking for the learning, and positive aspects of stressful or negative events, has been shown to:

- Improve physical health

- Reduce stress and depression

- Build confidence

- Strengthen relationships

- Increase the likelihood of achieving goals

Instructions

Please call to mind a recent misstep, setback, or disappointment, and write freely about all of the thoughts and feelings it triggered in you. It may be helpful to write from a third person perspective, such as with the positive voice you identified in exercise 17.

_____

_____

_____

_____

_____

_____

_____

_____

_____

_____

_____

_____

_____

_____

_____

_____

_____

_____

_____

Now take the perspective of a scientist who tries to learn all they can from a failed experiment. What happened and why did it happen? Where did things go off-track? What, specifically, derailed you?

_____

_____

_____

_____

_____

_____

_____

_____

_____

_____

_____

_____

_____

_____

_____

_____

_____

_____

_____

_____

_____

_____

What worked and what didn't?

_____

_____

_____

_____

_____

_____

_____

_____

_____

_____

_____

_____

What key insights have you learned from this experience? What will you try to do differently next time?

_____

_____

_____

_____

_____

_____

_____

_____

_____

Stressful, difficult, and even painful events can sometimes have positive—as well as negative—effects on us. Can you think of any ways that you—or your life—have changed in positive ways as a result of this experience? You may also describe future positive effects that could result from this experience.

_____

_____

_____

_____

_____

_____

_____

_____

_____

_____

_____

_____

_____

_____

_____

_____

_____

_____

_____

_____

_____

_____

_____

_____

_____

_____

_____

Tip

The meaning that you make out of a setback or negative experience strongly influences your recovery and how you respond. This exercise is not meant to minimize difficult events or the painful emotions they cause. Instead, it helps widen your perspective to include both the negative and positive effects of these events and what you can learn from them. This builds resiliency and will empower you to continue to move forward.

19. Channel Your Nerves

Strategies for Stressful Situations

Growing, learning, and working to achieve important goals often involves stepping out of your comfort zone. You may be called on to do things that are new, uncomfortable, or that stretch your skills, and this can be stressful and anxiety-provoking. This exercise will help you engage in positive self-talk when you are stressed in order to harness your stress response rather than getting bogged down by it.

Benefits

Recognizing the positive aspects of stress has been shown to:

- Build confidence and improve performance

- Help you recover from stress more quickly

- Buffer against the negative mental and physical effects of stress

Instructions

Please take a moment to think about the direction you want to go in your life and the steps you want to take in the upcoming month to continue to make progress toward your long-term goals. Is there a particular step or action that raises your anxiety or makes you feel stressed? This could be anything from asking others for help, to public speaking, to learning a new skill. Please describe a specific "next step" that you are nervous about.

_____

_____

_____

_____

_____

_____

_____

_____

The physiological signs of anxiety or nervousness—butterflies in the stomach, racing heart, quicker breath—are very similar to those of excitement. Reframing nervousness as excitement, by telling yourself, "I'm excited!" "I'm pumped!" or, "I'm psyched!" is an effective way to harness your nerves instead of worrying about them. Attempting to calm down (the physiological opposite of the stress response) is usually ineffective when you are in this heightened state, and takes mental resources away from the task at hand. This strategy is useful for acute stress situations, such as giving a presentation, rather than chronic stress or overwhelm. How can you reframe your nerves as excitement—in your own words—and put your nervous energy to good use?

_____

_____

_____

_____

Another helpful strategy is to remind yourself that you are capable of meeting the challenge you are facing. Please write about the internal and external resources you can draw upon to take the step that you identified above. Be your own coach, mentor, or cheerleader and offer yourself words of confidence and encouragement. What strengths do you have, and what previous experiences have you had that indicate you can handle this situation?

_____

_____

_____

_____

_____

_____

_____

_____

It can be stressful and uncomfortable to take challenging steps or move into new territory. The level of stress you experience is often a direct reflection of how much you care about something. Please take a moment to write about why you care about what you are doing. What are the values and meaning of the steps you are taking, that lie beneath the stress, fear, or nervousness?

_____

_____

_____

_____

_____

_____

_____

_____

_____

_____

_____

_____

_____

_____

_____

_____

_____

_____

_____

_____

_____

_____

When you need to stretch beyond your comfort zone and rise to a challenge, which of these three self-talk strategies do you think will be most useful to you, and why?

- Reframing nerves as excitement

- Reminding yourself that you are capable

- Connecting to the meaning beneath the nerves

_____

_____

_____

_____

_____

_____

_____

_____

_____

_____

How will you remember to use one or more of these strategies when you are nervous or stressed?

_____

_____

_____

What obstacles might get in the way of engaging in positive self-talk when you're nervous?

_____

_____

_____

What can you do to overcome these obstacles?

_____

_____

_____

Tip

Did you know that stress actually improves performance, as long as you're not stressed about being stressed? People who are nervous perform better than people who are relaxed or calm. What you tell yourself about stressful events shapes how you feel about them, how you respond, and how quickly you recover. The simple act of changing your story about stress can make a big difference to your emotional experience, and help you bring your best self to challenges.

This exercise is based on the work of Kelly McGonigal and Alison Brooks.

20. Re-write Your Story

The Hero's Journey

This exercise involves engaging in a fun creative writing exercise that will help you see yourself—and your goal—in a new light.

Benefits

This exercise has been shown to:

- Help people change limiting beliefs about themselves

- Build confidence and self-efficacy

- Improve self-image

- Increase persistence toward important goals

Instructions:

Step 1.

Please choose the following ingredients for your story:

- A hero, or protagonist. Identify a character of your choice to represent you. This could be an animal, the actor you would choose to play you in the movie of your life, your favorite superhero, etc.

_____

- A difficult challenge, goal or quest. What is the hero seeking? Please choose a fictional or metaphorical representation of an important goal you're working toward, or problem you are trying to address.

_____

_____

- One or more obstacles in the hero's quest. This could include a villain, or other forces or events that must be overcome.

_____

_____

_____

- Resources or assets. These can include mentors, helpers, guardian angels, secret knowledge, superpowers, etc.

_____

_____

_____

Now, please write—and/or draw—a story in the genre of your choice, describing your hero's life before the quest, how the quest took root and became important, and how your hero overcame the odds to reach their goal. What strengths, powers, or resources does your hero call upon for help? How do they manage to triumph in the end?

_____

_____

_____

_____

_____

_____

_____

_____

_____

_____

_____

_____

_____

_____

_____

_____

_____

_____

_____

_____

_____

_____

_____

_____

_____

_____

_____

_____

_____

_____

_____

_____

_____

_____

_____

_____

_____

_____

_____

_____

_____

_____

If the hero were to give you one piece of wisdom, advice, or encouragement, what would it be?

_____

_____

_____

This exercise is based on the work of Joseph Campbell and Lewis Mehl-Madrona.

21. Check-In

Congratulations! You've been working to make progress on the things you care about and have learned some strategies for dealing with the challenges and setbacks that occur along the way. Please take a moment to think back over what you've done, what it's been like, and the impact the exercises have had on you. If you like, you can flip back through the journal to refresh your memory.

What has the process of completing these exercises—and working toward your goals—been like for you?

_____

_____

_____

_____

_____

What progress have you made toward your goals? What have you learned, or how have you changed as a result of the work you are doing?

_____

_____

_____

_____

_____

_____

_____

_____

_____

_____

_____

_____

How are you feeling about your goals and the progress you are making?

_____

_____

_____

_____

_____

What would you like to say or do to acknowledge, affirm, and celebrate your efforts?

_____

_____

_____

chapter

4

Sustaining

Any goal that is worth achieving requires effort, and big goals require sustained effort over time. We can lose motivation when progress is slow, or difficult to see, as it often is. People often give up if the effort becomes too strenuous, or downright boring, and the rewards are few and far between. This series of exercises offers strategies to sustain your energy and maintain momentum.

22. Set a Mini Goal

This exercise involves setting a small goal that you can accomplish in 15-30 minutes, that you will do within the week. Because mini-goals are small, they are easy to achieve, and build a sense of competence and control. Accomplishing a goal triggers a burst dopamine, which generates positive emotion and reinforces forward momentum.

Benefits

Goal-setting has been shown to:

- Help generate movement and momentum

- Reduce inertia, anxiety and depression

- Provide a sense of control and accomplishment

- Prioritize what is important to you

Instructions

Please identify one thing that you would like to do today, or within the week, that can be completed in 15-30 minutes. If you have a larger goal in mind, break it down into small steps and choose one to work on. Please describe your mini-goal:

_____

_____

_____

What made you choose this particular goal? What impact do you think completing will have on you and/or others?

_____

_____

_____

_____

_____

When will you do it?

_____

Where will you do it?

_____

How will you do it? Please describe the steps you will take to complete this goal.

_____

_____

_____

23. Connect to Your Values

This exercise involves reflecting on the values that are most important to you, and how they relate to your goals.

Benefits

Reflecting on your values has been shown to:

- Improve mental and physical health

- Boost academic performance and increase work satisfaction, engagement, and effectiveness

- Increase confidence, sense of control, and ability to manage stress

- Increase sense of connection and empathy

- Strengthen motivation and follow-through on personal goals

Instructions

Please take a moment to reflect on the things that you care about most. Choose 3 values that feel important to you right now, either from the list on the next page, or you may add your own. You may pick values that are existing strengths or ones that you aspire to and would like to develop in yourself.

What 3 values feel most important to you in your life right now?

1. _____

2. _____

3. _____

Abundance	Environment	Intelligence
Accountability	Equality	Intensity
Accuracy	Excellence	Intimacy
Achievement	Exploration	Intuition
Adventure	Fairness	Joy
Authenticity	Faith	Justice
Autonomy	Faithfulness	Knowledge
Balance	Family	Leadership
Beauty	Flair	Learning
Caring	Flexibility	Love
Challenge	Forgiveness	Loyalty
Change	Freedom	Meaning
Clarity	Friendship	Merit
Cleanliness/Orderliness	Frugality	Moderation
Collaboration	Fulfillment	Modesty
Commitment	Fun	Nature
Communication	Generosity	Nurturing
Community	Genuineness	Open-mindedness
Compassion	Good will	Openness
Competence	Goodness	Optimism
Confidence	Gratitude	Patriotism
Connection	Hard work	Peace/Non-violence
Conservation	Harmony	Perseverance
Cooperation	Healing	Personal growth
Courage	Health	Pleasure
Creativity	Holistic Living	Positive impact
Credibility	Honesty	Power/Influence
Decisiveness	Honor	Practicality
Democracy	Improvement	Preservation
Determination	Independence	Problem-solving
Discipline	Individuality	Professionalism
Discovery	Initiative	Progress
Diversity	Inner peace	Prosperity
Education	Innovation	Punctuality
Efficiency	Integrity	Purpose

Quantity over quality	Self-esteem	Straightforwardness
Reciprocity	Self-expression	Strength
Recognition	Self-improvement	Success
Relaxation	Self-love	Systemization
Reliability	Self-mastery	Teamwork
Resourcefulness	Self-reliance	Timeliness
Respect for others	Self-trust	Tradition
Responsibility	Sensuality	Tranquility
Responsiveness	Service	Trust
Results	Simplicity	Trustworthiness
Romance	Sincerity	Truth
Sacrifice	Skill	Unity
Safety	Solitude	Variety
Satisfying others	Speed	Vitality
Security	Spirituality	Vulnerability
Self-awareness	Stability	Wealth
Self-confidence	Status	Wisdom

Next, please choose one of your top 3 values, and write freely for 10 minutes about why this value is important to you.

How is this value related to your goals and the direction you want to be going in your life?

_____

_____

_____

_____

_____

_____

_____

_____

_____

_____

_____

_____

_____

_____

_____

_____

_____

_____

_____

_____

_____

_____

_____

How do you express this value in your daily life, including what you did this week? If this is an aspirational value, how would you like to express it in your daily life?

_____

_____

_____

_____

_____

_____

_____

_____

_____

How would you like to express this value in the future?

_____

_____

_____

_____

_____

_____

_____

_____

_____

Tip

We often get caught up in day-to-day activities and concerns and our values fade into the background. A small reminder—such as a word or image on a bracelet, a note, or the wallpaper on your phone or computer—can keep an important value at the forefront of your mind. This simple practice has been shown to magnify and prolong the benefits of reflecting on your values.

This exercise is based on research by Geoffrey Cohen and David Sherman.

24. Celebrate Progress

We have the tendency to focus our attention on things that are going poorly, and when we do accomplish something positive, we may simply cross it off the list and move on to the next thing. This does little to reinforce our forward momentum! This exercise will help you acknowledge the steps you are taking—not just the results—and celebrate small wins, which fuels the motivation to keep going.

Benefits

Recognizing and celebrating progress has been shown to:

- Improve self-concept and boost happiness

- Reinforce forward momentum and follow-through

- Reduce stress and fatigue

Instructions:

Strategy #1: What Went Well, and Why?

This exercise helps to correct our natural negative mental skew toward setbacks, what we're anxious about, or what is going wrong, and shift to a more positive perspective, which fuels the motivation to keep moving forward. Please take a moment to look back over the past week. What went well—particularly in relationship to your goal—and why did it go well? Please list 3 things.

_____

_____

_____

_____

_____

_____

_____

_____

_____

Strategy #2: Celebrate!

It's important to pause and acknowledge the progress you've made, even if the gains are incremental. It's even more important to celebrate the efforts you have made rather than focusing exclusively on results. For example, you might decide to reward yourself for every five jobs you apply for, rather than waiting until you land a job to celebrate. Celebrating your actions, which you have control over, can reinforce continued action more reliably than celebrating outcomes. Please take a moment to write about some of the positive steps you've taken toward your goals.

_____

_____

_____

_____

_____

How can you acknowledge, celebrate, or reward yourself for the work you've done so far?

_____

_____

_____

The What Went Well and Why exercise is based on research by Martin Seligman.

25. Make Time

Many of us suffer from chronic busyness and feel stretched just keeping up with the things that need to be done day-to-day. It can be a real challenge to carve out additional time to invest in goals, growth, or change. Yet how you spend your time is how you spend your life, and it can be valuable to periodically assess whether you are prioritizing the things that are meaningful to you. This exercise will help you evaluate how you spend your time and offer strategies to create more time for the things you care about.

Benefits

Making conscious choices about how you spend your time has been shown to:

- Reduce stress and overwhelm

- Improve work/life satisfaction and fulfillment

- Increase effectiveness, productivity and impact

Instructions

Please take a moment to think about what you want to focus on in the next month. What is important to you? How do you want to spend your time? Please list everything you'd like to do and briefly elaborate on each heading. For example, Relationships: have quality family time, hang out with friends, join a class or club to meet new people.

1. _____

   _____

2. _____

   _____

3. _____

   _____

4. _____

   _____

5. _____

_____

6. _____

_____

7. _____

_____

8. _____

_____

9. _____

_____

10. _____

_____

11. _____

_____

12. _____

_____

13. _____

_____

14. _____

_____

15. _____

_____

Next, please assign each category or item on the list a rough percentage. How much of your total time available would you like to spend on each area?

Now think back on how you actually spent your time over the last week. Please list everything you did, and assign a rough percentage (time you spent of your total time available) to each category or item.

1. _____

_____

2. _____

_____

3. _____

_____

4. _____

_____

5. _____

_____

6. _____

_____

7. _____

_____

8. _____

_____

9. _____

_____

10. _____

_____

11. _____

_____

12. _____

_____

13. _____

_____

14. _____

_____

15. _____

_____

How do the two lists compare? What does the alignment—and misalignment—of your two lists bring up for you?

_____

_____

_____

_____

_____

_____

_____

_____

_____

_____

You may be familiar with the 80/20 principle, which states that a small percentage of input or effort leads to a large percentage of results. For example, 20% of customers generate 80% of a company's profit, 20% of products generate 80% of the sales, and so on. Concentrating on expanding the top 20%, rather than investing in all customers and products equally, can lead to exponential gains. This principle can be applied to all aspects of life, and it can be helpful to look at your time through this lens. When you think about how you spend your time, what activities generate the most enjoyment, meaning, or other outcomes that are most important to you? For example, what specific family activities make you feel most connected? What specific work activities have the most impact?

Please look over the list of how you spent your time in the last week. Identify the top three time investments that lead to the kind of experiences and emotions you want more of.

1. _____

2. _____

3. _____

When, where, and how can you do more of these things?

_____

_____

_____

Now identify the things on your list that give you the least return (however you define it) on your time investment.

1. _____

2. _____

3. _____

What can you let go of, or how can you do less of these things?

_____

_____

_____

How and when will you let go of these activities?

_____

_____

_____

Tip

Did you know that the experience of time pressure stems from our attitudes about time as much as from actual demands on our time? Feeling in control of our own time can have a big impact. The simple act of shifting your mindset from "I have to..." to "I choose to...", and why, can reduce time scarcity. For example, "I choose to go grocery shopping because I want to have healthy food options at home."

26. Give Yourself a Break

Our minds and bodies are designed to alternate between spending and recovering energy, in roughly 90-minute cycles. It is impossible to sustain energy and focus for long periods of time, and if working toward your goal becomes tedious, overwhelming, or exhausting, you are much more likely to give up. Taking regular breaks to relax, replenish your energy, and have fun is essential to maintaining motivation and to getting more done, more sustainably. Longer periods of rest, such as a good night's sleep, a leisurely weekend, or a vacation, are also essential to restoring energy and giving your mind time to rest.

Benefits

Taking regular breaks and engaging in replenishing activities has been shown to:

- Reduce stress, anxiety and fatigue

- Improve physical health and allow your body to recuperate from stress

- Improve focus, memory and learning

- Enhance efficiency and productivity

Instructions

Rather than trying to manage your time and fit everything in, think about how you can manage (replenish and sustain) your energy. Please identify five activities that you could do to take quick work breaks during the day to relax, have fun, and restore your energy.

1. _____

2. _____

3. _____

4. _____

5. _____

Please identify three longer activities that you find restorative, that you could do in the evening or on weekends.

1. _____

2. _____

3. _____

Which of these activities would like to practice this week?

_____

When, where and how will you do it?

_____

_____

_____

Tip

People who work steadily—in small, regular increments—are far more likely to meet their goals than people who work in spurts or those who put in long hours. For example, authors who write one page per day publish more books than those who attempt to get a lot done in one sitting. If your work requires sustained focus, working in longer than 90-minute stretches or for more than 4 total hours per day is likely to be counterproductive.

27. Solidify Your Commitment

This exercise involves sharing a specific commitment to action, as well as passing on what you have learned from this process.

Benefits

Sharing your goals, knowledge, and experience with other people has been shown to:

- Solidify commitment and increase follow-through

- Reinforce learning

- Increase happiness and improve self-concept

Instructions

Please take a moment to think about your direction and what you would like to accomplish over the next few months. How do you want to continue to grow? What are your next steps? Choose a commitment that you'd like to share publicly by creating an "I will" pledge. This could be a specific action you'd like to take, a goal, or an important learning you'd like to remember in the future. For example, "I will read 10 pages a day," "I will make time for my friends," or "I will remember that things get easier with practice."

I will _____

_____

_____

Are you ready to solidify your commitment by sharing it publicly? If so, please share your pledge to our Facebook page tinyurl.com/actualizers If you like, you can post a selfie with your pledge.

Next, please think back to where you started at the beginning of this journal, and what this process has been like for you. What words of wisdom, support, and encouragement would have been helpful to you in this journey?

_____

_____

_____

_____

_____

What have you learned that you can pass on to others? What support and encouragement can you offer to people who want to work toward important goals? If you feel comfortable, you may post this to our Facebook page as well. We would love to hear from you.

_____

_____

_____

_____

_____

_____

_____

_____

_____

Tip

Did you know that most people want to maintain a consistent image of themselves? This means that when you publicly share a belief, value, or commitment, you are more likely to behave in ways that are consistent with what you have presented. You can use this to your advantage by sharing specific things about yourself that you want to live up to.

28. Check-In

Congratulations, you made it through the journal! Hopefully you have learned some useful strategies and have made progress on goals that are important to you.

Please take a moment to reflect on where you started and how far you have come.

_____

_____

_____

_____

_____

What have you learned? How have you grown or changed as a result of completing these exercises? What impact has this had on you and on your life?

_____

_____

_____

_____

_____

_____

_____

_____

_____

_____

_____

_____

_____

Looking Forward

At the start of this journal you spent some time thinking about what you wanted for your future. This can change over time and it's important to periodically check-in with yourself about your direction.

Please take a moment to reflect on your hopes for the future and describe the kind of person you hope to become and the kind of impact you hope to have.

What do you want your work, family, educational, social and personal life to look like?

_____

_____

_____

_____

_____

_____

_____

_____

_____

_____

_____

_____

_____

_____

_____

_____

_____

_____

_____

_____

_____

_____

What do you see as the next steps you need to take to pursue these goals?

Working to realize your hopes, dreams, and goals is a lifelong process. A number of blank note pages have been included for you to continue to write down your thoughts and plans, or to repeat exercises that you found to be particularly helpful or enjoyable. Feel free to experiment and adapt the exercises to suit your needs. I wish you all the best on your continued journey!

If you would like to share any of your experiences or feedback with the author, you may email your comments to jessica@growingwellness.life or post to the Actualizers community Facebook page tinyurl.com/actualizers. Please note that while I read every email and enjoy hearing about people's experiences, I am unable to respond to every one. I would also greatly appreciate an Amazon review, which helps other people to find the journal.

Notes

Notes

Notes

Actualize!

Notes

Notes

References

WHAT'S SO GREAT ABOUT GOALS?

Korb, A. (2016). The upward spiral: using neuroscience to reverse the course of depression, one small change at a time. Strawberry Hills, NSW: ReadHowYouWant.

Miller, C. A. (2017). Getting grit: The evidence-based approach to cultivating passion, perseverance, and purpose. Boulder, Col.: Sounds True.

EXPECTED BENEFITS

Duckworth, A. (2016) Grit: The power of passion and perseverance. New York: Scribner.

Dweck, C. S. (2006). Mindset: The new psychology of success. New York: Random House.

Kamenetz, A. (2015, July 10). The Writing Assignment That Changes Lives. Retrieved from https://www.npr.org/sections/ed/2015/07/10/419202925/the-writing-assignment-that-changes-lives

Korb, A. (2016). The upward spiral: using neuroscience to reverse the course of depression, one small change at a time. Strawberry Hills, NSW: ReadHowYouWant.

McGonigal, K. (2015). The upside of stress: Why stress is good for you, and how to get good at it. New York: Penguin Random House.

Neff, K. (2011) Self-Compassion: The Proven Power of Being Kind to Yourself. New York: HarperCollins.\

Schippers, M. C., Scheepers, A. W., & Peterson, J. B. (2015). A scalable goal-setting intervention closes both the gender and ethnic minority achievement gap. Palgrave Communications, 1(1). doi:10.1057/palcomms.2015.14

Searing, L. (2014, October 06). Learning that social lives and personalities change in high school may help teens avoid depression. Retrieved from https://www.washingtonpost.com/national/health-science/teens-taught-that-personality-traits-change-in-high-school-cope-with-depression-better/2014/10/06/723fb3b2-4a44-11e4-a046-120a8a855cca_story.html

1. ADOPT A MINDSET FOR SUCCESS

Dweck, C. S. (2006). Mindset: The new psychology of success. New York: Random House.

McGonigal, K. (2015). The upside of stress: Why stress is good for you, and how to get good at it. New York: Penguin Random House.

Mehl-Madrona, L., & Mainguy, B. (2015). Remapping your mind: The neuroscience of self-transformation through story. Rochester: Bear & Company.

Yeager, D.S. & Dweck, C.S. (2012). Mindsets that promote resilience: When students believe that personal characteristics can be developed. Educational Psychologist, 47, 1-13.

2. DREAM BIG: IDENTIFY A LARGER-THAN-SELF GOAL

Crocker, J., Olivier, M., & Nuer, N. (2009). Self-image Goals and Compassionate Goals: Costs and Benefits. Self and Identity, 8(2-3), 251-269. doi:10.1080/15298860802505160

McGonigal, K. (2015). The upside of stress: Why stress is good for you, and how to get good at it. New York: Penguin Random House.

Yeager, D. S., Henderson, M. D., Paunesku, D., Walton, G. M., D'mello, S., Spitzer, B. J., & Duckworth, A. L. (2014). Boring but important: A self-transcendent purpose for learning fosters academic self-regulation. Journal of Personality and Social Psychology, 107(4), 559-580.

3. PICTURE YOUR FUTURE: WHAT DO YOU WANT?

Miller, C. A. (2017). Getting grit: The evidence-based approach to cultivating passion, perseverance, and purpose. Boulder, Col.: Sounds True.

Schippers, M. C., Scheepers, A. W., & Peterson, J. B. (2015). A scalable goal-setting intervention closes both the gender and ethnic minority achievement gap. Palgrave Communications, 1(1). doi:10.1057/palcomms.2015.14

4. VISIT THE FUTURE: BEST AND WORST CASE SCENARIOS

Schippers, M. C., Scheepers, A. W., & Peterson, J. B. (2015). A scalable goal-setting intervention closes both the gender and ethnic minority achievement gap. Palgrave Communications, 1(1). doi:10.1057/palcomms.2015.14

Lyubomirsky, S., & Kurtz, J. (2013). Positively happy: routes to sustainable happiness; a six week course. Milwaukie, Or.: Positive Acorn.

Miller, C. A. (2017). Getting grit: The evidence-based approach to cultivating passion, perseverance, and purpose. Boulder, Col.: Sounds True.

Oettingen, G. (2014). Rethinking positive thinking: Inside the new science of motivation. New York: Current.

5. MAP IT OUT: IDENTIFY YOUR ROUTE

Schippers, M. C., Scheepers, A. W., & Peterson, J. B. (2015). A scalable goal-setting intervention closes both the gender and ethnic minority achievement gap. Palgrave Communications, 1(1). doi:10.1057/palcomms.2015.14

Mehl-Madrona, L., & Mainguy, B. (2015). Remapping your mind: The neuroscience of self-transformation through story. Rochester: Bear & Company.

6. ENGAGE YOUR STRENGTHS

Achor, S. (2010). The happiness advantage: The seven principles of positive psychology that fuel success and performance at work. New York: Broadway Books.

Haidt, J. (2006). The happiness hypothesis: Putting ancient wisdom and philosophy to the test of modern science. London: Arrow.

Seligman, M. E. (2011) Flourish: A Visionary New Understanding of Happiness and Well-being. New York: Free Press.

7. CHECK-IN

Amabile, T., & Kramer, S. (2011). The progress principle: Using small wins to ignite joy, engagement, and creativity at work. Boston, MA: Harvard Business Review Press.

Pennebaker, J. W. (1997). Opening up: The healing power of expressing emotions. New York: Guildford Press.

8. SET A MINI GOAL

Amabile, T., & Kramer, S. (2011). The progress principle: Using small wins to ignite joy, engagement, and creativity at work. Boston, MA: Harvard Business Review Press.

Medina, J. (2008). Brain rules: 12 principles for surviving and thriving at work, home, and school. Seattle, WA: Pear Press.

Patterson, K. (2011). Change anything: The new science of personal success. New York: Business Plus.

9. WOOP IT!

Oettingen, G. (2014). Rethinking positive thinking: Inside the new science of motivation. New York: Current.

Pennebaker, J. W. (1997). Opening up: The healing power of expressing emotions. New York: Guildford Press.

10. MAKE IT MANAGEABLE

Amabile, T., & Kramer, S. (2011). The progress principle: Using small wins to ignite joy, engagement, and creativity at work. Boston, MA: Harvard Business Review Press.

McGonigal, K. (2012). The Willpower Instinct: How Self-Control Works, Why It Matters, and What You Can Do to Get More of It. New York, NY: Avery.

Oettingen, G. (2014). Rethinking positive thinking: Inside the new science of motivation. New York: Current.

Patterson, K. (2011). Change anything: The new science of personal success. New York: Business Plus.

Service, O. G. (2018). Think Small: The surprisingly simple ways to reach big goals. S.l.: Michael Omara Books.

11. HARNESS THE POWER OF HABIT

Achor, S. (2010). The happiness advantage: The seven principles of positive psychology that fuel success and performance at work. New York: Broadway Books.

Clear, J. (2019). Atomic Habits: An Easy and Proven Way to Build Good Habits and Break Bad Ones. London: Cornerstone.

Duhigg, C. (2014). The power of habit: why we do what we do in life and business. New York: Random House Trade Paperbacks.

McGonigal, K. (2012). The Willpower Instinct: How Self-Control Works, Why It Matters, and What You Can Do to Get More of It. New York, NY: Avery.

12. TRACK IT!

Clear, J. (2019). Atomic Habits: An Easy and Proven Way to Build Good Habits and Break Bad Ones. London: Cornerstone.

Rubin, G. (2009). The happiness project: Or why I spent a year trying to sing in the morning, clean my closets, fight right, read Aristotle, and generally have more fun. New York, NY: Harper.

13: GET SUPPORT

Duhigg, C. (2014). The power of habit: why we do what we do in life and business. New York: Random House Trade Paperbacks.

Patterson, K. (2011). Change anything: The new science of personal success. New York: Business Plus.

Service, O. G. (2018). Think Small: The surprisingly simple ways to reach big goals. S.l.: Michael Omara Books.

14. CHECK-IN

Amabile, T., & Kramer, S. (2011). The progress principle: Using small wins to ignite joy, engagement, and creativity at work. Boston, MA: Harvard Business Review Press.

Pennebaker, J. W. (1997). Opening up: The healing power of expressing emotions. New York: Guildford Press.

15. SET A MINI GOAL

Amabile, T., & Kramer, S. (2011). The progress principle: Using small wins to ignite joy, engagement, and creativity at work. Boston, MA: Harvard Business Review Press.

Medina, J. (2008). Brain rules: 12 principles for surviving and thriving at work, home, and school. Seattle, WA: Pear Press.

Patterson, K. (2011). Change anything: The new science of personal success. New York: Business Plus.

16. CHANGE YOUR SELF-TALK

Achor, S. (2010). The happiness advantage: The seven principles of positive psychology that fuel success and performance at work. New York: Broadway Books.

Goulston, M., & Ferrazzi, K. (2010). Just Listen. New York, NY: AMACOM.

Harris, R. (2011). The Confidence Gap: A guide to overcoming fear and self-doubt. Boston: Trumpeter.

Kay, K. S. (2014). The Confidence Code: The science and art of self-assurance—what women should know. New York: HarperCollins.

McGonigal, K. (2012). The Willpower Instinct: How Self-Control Works, Why It Matters, and What You Can Do to Get More of It. New York, NY: Avery.

17. PRACTICE SELF-COMPASSION

McGonigal, K. (2012). The Willpower Instinct: How Self-Control Works, Why It Matters, and What You Can Do to Get More of It. New York, NY: Avery.

Mehl-Madrona, L. (2010). Healing the mind through the power of story: The promise of narrative psychiatry. Rochester, VT: Bear & Company.

Neff, K. (2011) Self-Compassion: The Proven Power of Being Kind to Yourself. New York: HarperCollins.

18. BE A SCIENTIST

McGonigal, K. (2015). The upside of stress: Why stress is good for you, and how to get good at it. New York: Penguin Random House.

Patterson, K. (2011). Change anything: The new science of personal success. New York: Business Plus.

Pennebaker, J. W. (1997). Opening up: The healing power of expressing emotions. New York: Guildford Press.

19. CHANNEL YOUR NERVES

Brooks, A. W. (2014). Get excited: Reappraising pre-performance anxiety as excitement. Journal of Experimental Psychology: General, 143(3), 1144-1158. doi:10.1037/a0035325

Jamieson, J. P., Mendes, W. B., Blackstock, E., & Schmader, T. (2010). Turning the knots in your stomach into bows: Reappraising arousal improves performance on the GRE. Journal of Experimental Social Psychology, 46(1), 208-212. doi:10.1016/j.jesp.2009.08.015

McGonigal, K. (n.d.). How to make stress your friend. Retrieved February 27, 2017, from https://www.ted.com/talks/kelly_mcgonigal_how_to_make_stress_your_friend

McGonigal, K. (2015). The upside of stress: Why stress is good for you, and how to get good at it. New York: Penguin Random House.

20. RE-WRITE YOUR STORY

Mehl-Madrona, L. (2010). Healing the mind through the power of story: The promise of narrative psychiatry. Rochester, VT: Bear & Company.

Mehl-Madrona, L., & Mainguy, B. (2015). Remapping your mind: The neuroscience of self-transformation through story. Rochester: Bear & Company.

Pennebaker, J. W. (2013). Writing to heal: A guided journal for recovering from trauma and emotional upheaval. Wheat Ridge, CO: Center for Journal Therapy.

Smith, E. E. (2017). The power of meaning: Crafting a life that matters. London: Rider Books.

21. CHECK-IN

Amabile, T., & Kramer, S. (2011). The progress principle: Using small wins to ignite joy, engagement, and creativity at work. Boston, MA: Harvard Business Review Press.

Pennebaker, J. W. (1997). Opening up: The healing power of expressing emotions. New York: Guildford Press.

22. SET A MINI GOAL

Amabile, T., & Kramer, S. (2011). The progress principle: Using small wins to ignite joy, engagement, and creativity at work. Boston, MA: Harvard Business Review Press.

Medina, J. (2008). Brain rules: 12 principles for surviving and thriving at work, home, and school. Seattle, WA: Pear Press.

Patterson, K. (2011). Change anything: The new science of personal success. New York: Business Plus.

23. CONNECT TO YOUR VALUES

Cohen, G. L., & Sherman, D. K. (2014). The Psychology of Change: Self-Affirmation and Social Psychological Intervention. Annual Review of Psychology, 65(1), 333-371. doi:10.1146/annurev-psych-010213-115137

Duckworth, A. (2016) Grit: The power of passion and perseverance. New York: Scribner

McGonigal, K. (2015). The upside of stress: Why stress is good for you, and how to get good at it. New York: Penguin Random House.

Miller, W. R., & Rollnick, S. (2013). Motivational interviewing: Helping people change. London: The Guilford Press.

Patterson, K. (2011). Change anything: The new science of personal success. New York: Business Plus.

Sinek, S. (2013). Start with why: how great leaders inspire everyone to take action. London: Portfolio/Penguin.

24. CELEBRATE PROGRESS

Duhigg, C. (2014). The power of habit: why we do what we do in life and business. New York: Random House Trade Paperbacks.

Lyubomirsky, S. (2008). The how of happiness: A scientific approach to getting the life you want. New York: Penguin Press.

Seligman, M. E. (2011) Flourish: A Visionary New Understanding of Happiness and Well-being. New York: Free Press.

Seligman, M. E., Steen, T. A., Park, N., & Peterson, C. (2005). Positive Psychology Progress: Empirical Validation of Interventions. American Psychologist, 60(5), 410-421. doi:10.1037/0003-066x.60.5.410

Service, O. G. (2018). Think Small: The surprisingly simple ways to reach big goals. S.l.: Michael Omara Books.

25. MAKE TIME

Koch, R. (2018). The 80/20 principle: The secret of achieving more with less. New York: Currency.

Rechtschaffen, S. (2002). Time shifting: Creating more time to enjoy your life. New York: Broadway Books.

Why You Never Seem to Have Enough Time. (2019, March 13). Retrieved from http://thehappyquotient.com/2019/03/13/why-you-never-seem-to-have-enough-time/

26. GIVE YOURSELF A BREAK

Schwartz, T. (2013, February 09). Relax! You'll Be More Productive. Retrieved July 12, 2017, from http://www.nytimes.com/2013/02/10/opinion/sunday/relax-youll-be-more-productive.html

McCarthy, T. S., William Oncken, Jr. and Donald L. Wass, Ghoshal, H. B., & Mankins, M. C. (2015, July 16). Manage Your Energy, Not Your Time. Retrieved December 18, 2017, from https://hbr.org/2007/10/manage-your-energy-not-your-time

27. SOLIDIFY YOUR COMMITMENT

Service, O. G. (2018). Think Small: The surprisingly simple ways to reach big goals. S.l.: Michael Omara Books.

Schippers, M. C., Scheepers, A. W., & Peterson, J. B. (2015). A scalable goal-setting intervention closes both the gender and ethnic minority achievement gap. Palgrave Communications, 1(1). doi:10.1057/palcomms.2015.14

Walton, G. M., & Cohen, G. L. (2011). A Brief Social-Belonging Intervention Improves Academic and Health Outcomes of Minority Students. Science, 331(6023), 1447-1451. doi:10.1126/science.1198364

28. CHECK-IN

Amabile, T., & Kramer, S. (2011). The progress principle: Using small wins to ignite joy, engagement, and creativity at work. Boston, MA: Harvard Business Review Press.

Medina, J. (2008). Brain rules: 12 principles for surviving and thriving at work, home, and school. Seattle, WA: Pear Press.

Pennebaker, J. W. (1997). Opening up: The healing power of expressing emotions. New York: Guildford Press.

Made in the USA
Middletown, DE
03 July 2019